More Than Four Questions
Inviting Children's Voices to the Seder
A CONVERSATIONAL HAGGADAH COMPANION

Sharon Black
with the wisdom of children

Ben Yehuda Press
Teaneck, New Jersey

Published by Ben Yehuda Press
122 Ayers Court #1B
Teaneck, NJ 07666

http://www.BenYehudaPress.com

To subscribe to our monthly book club and support independent Jewish publishing, visit patreon.com/BenYehudaPress

ISBN13 978-1-963475-42-5

20 21 22 / 10 9 8 7 6 5 4 3b   2030331

For my mom, Enid Black,
and her father, Abraham Silverman, z"l,
through whom my love for seder and all things Jewish flourished.

"Why do we open the door for Elijah? Can't he just come in?"

—Daniella, age 11

OPENING THE DOOR:
How to use this book

"It is an old saying, ask a Jew a question, and the Jew answers with a question. Every answer given arouses new questions. The progress of knowledge is matched by an increase in the hidden and mysterious."
—Rabbi Leo Baeck

The Torah gives the earliest instructions for what is now called experiential Jewish education.

Sacrifice a paschal lamb, commands the Torah, and eat matzah for seven days.

And when your child asks why — or even if she doesn't — explain that "this is because of what God did for me when I came out of Egypt" (Exodus 13:8).

This, of course, is the root of the Passover Seder.

While the seder was designed to spark children's questions, the fact is that for many of our children, the seder is often an opportunity to contribute what has been previously learned, whether by reciting the four questions or explaining sections of the Haggadah, rather than the chance for new discovery.

This book, MORE THAN FOUR QUESTIONS, accepts the reality that on Passover our children come back from school wanting to share with us what they have learned.

They are often not asking us, their parents, questions.

So let's turn around and ask them questions instead.

This book is a compilation of children's questions about Passover, asked over my many years teaching. I then posed the questions back to children ages five to sixteen. I met with them in small groups to think, question, and explore the inquiries together. In creating a warm, supportive, non-judgmental setting where it was safe for everyone to speak freely, an exciting interchange occurred eliciting many varied responses. I accepted all comments with respect and reflected back what I heard as a way of validating the children's opinions.

As we spoke, children exclaimed, "This is fun. We feel like we have a chance to let our brains fly out of our heads." At one of the discussion groups, Talia Cohen, said, "We have so much to say we'll be here until the morning prayers," making reference to the rabbis in the Haggadah who discussed Yitziat Mitzraim, the exodus from Egypt, until it was daybreak.

You will find children's inquiries on one side of the page. The wonderings and wisdom of children are located on the back of each question. No one answer is correct; the responses express different perspectives. Next to each child's answer is their name and age.

Rabbi Shlomo Carlebach said children led the way through the Red Sea. Here too, children's questions and insights can lead the way. Their open engagement bring the questions alive, inviting you too to interact. They can be a springboard for your own queries and of those gathered with you.

Before reading the children's responses, share one of the questions at your table.

What are other people's answers, thoughts, and understanding?

Which ideas hold meaning for them?

What new questions are generated from the discussion?

To enhance the conversation, thought-provoking queries geared for teenagers and adults are at the bottom of the page with each springboard question. Quotes and sources are on the other side of the page below the children's responses. On some pages, a note will indicate that further reflections for that question are located at the back of the book.

MORE THAN FOUR QUESTIONS is a book for children but not only for children. It speaks to varying ages of people, from the youngest sitting with you to the oldest. There are six sections: Preparing For Passover, Beginning The Seder, The Story, The Meal, Moving Toward Completion, and Further Reflections. It is sequentially grouped this way to make it easy to use as an accompaniment to a Haggadah.

I suggest you read through MORE THAN FOUR QUESTIONS before your gathering. Note the questions, comments, and reflections that resonate for you and that you would like to share. Consider which pages are good conversation starters for the group with whom you will be sharing this year's seder.

Using questioning as a vehicle of exploration delivers the message that asking is valued. In asking open-ended questions like, "Do you think freedom is the absence of slavery?" or "What would you like to learn from and discuss with Moses if you met him?" expansive thinking can emerge. A closed-ended question that can be answered with a simple yes or no, such as, "Do you like Passover?" doesn't enhance dialogue and engender contemplation. Try presenting forced analogies — putting two things together that don't normally go together — as a way to help jumpstart broad thinking. For example: How is a seder like a journey through time, a seder plate like a map, or breaking the matzah like knowing something needs to be fixed? Seder night is an especially propitious time to reflect, question, and freely converse.

At some point, you can add your own and others' inquiries and thoughts in the space provided, further making this book your own.

Perhaps in the busy pre-Passover days before the sedarim your children or grandchildren can occupy themselves by writing or drawing their responses in this book.

It has been suggested (Lubavitch Haggadah) that the questions of a child find a special echo in heaven, and so on Passover, reverberating in this world and beyond, is the chant of children across the globe asking, "Ma nishtanah ha-lailah ha-zeh meekol ha-lailot?" Why is this night different from all other nights?

May you and all those with you be blessed to ask questions along with the children and to experience this night as different.

Preparing For Passover

What is your favorite memory of Passover?

Why is Passover so important?

In what important ways do you celebrate your identity?

Why is Passover so important?

"It's important to pass down the story to the next generation and to get together with family." —Alix, 14

"You do unusual and fun customs." —Amram, 7

"It's in our circle of holidays and it's the beginning of the life of the Jewish people." —Yitzy, 6

"We celebrate our freedom and we tell the story to tell how great God is and how He saved us. We wouldn't be where we are today if He didn't save us. We remember that what happened was magical because we were living in miracles." —Toba, 8

"We are a small nation and we've been persecuted a lot in the past, so it's really a celebration of our freedom and an acknowledgement of it." —Avital, 15

"It's a good time to get together with everybody and talk together with everyone about how you feel about Pesach. There's a mitzvah to talk." —Davida, 9

"It's a chance to remember both how we felt when we were climbing out of Egypt and to tell the story of our leaving." —Drew, 6

"The Exodus from Egypt is a great foundation and mighty pillar of our Torah and our faith. We constantly repeat in our blessings and prayers, 'a remembrance of the Exodus from Egypt.' This pivotal event serves as absolute proof that God created the world. He is the original God who desires and is able to bring all things into being and He has the power to change His creations at any given time. And that is exactly what He did in Egypt. God changed the nature of the world for the Jewish people." —Sefer HaChinuch, 21

Why is a seder called a seder?

When has order or structure freed you?

Why is a seder called a seder?

"The story of our becoming free didn't just happen haphazardly. There was a sequence. So we mirror that and tell the story of our slavery and how we became free through the seder, which is also a sequence." —Avital, 15

"What's that song we sing that tells us what comes next in the seder?" —Noa, 6

"How does it go? Oh yeah — kadesh, u'rechatz, karpas, yachatz, maggid, rachtzah, motzi - matzah, maror, korech, shulchan orech, tzafun, barech, hallel, nirtzah. Those are all the parts." —Yitzy, 6

"What does that mean?" —Jade, 11

"It's Hebrew for: make kiddush, wash our hands without a blessing, dip celery in saltwater, break the middle matzah, tell the story of Passover, wash our hands with a blessing, say the blessing for matzah - eat matzah, eat bitter herbs, eat a matzah-bitter herb sandwich, have the meal, find the afikoman, say the blessings after the meal, sing songs of thanks, and finish the seder and hope we'll be in Jerusalem next year." —Elana, 9

The word seder means order. The Haggadah takes us through a fifteen step process carrying us from slavery to freedom. There were also fifteen steps leading to the inner courtyard of the Holy Temple in Jerusalem. They let us "go up" (*aliyah*) to the Temple. Here too, we are guided through the seder's fifteen steps, allowing us to "go up."

Why do we have a seder?

When have you felt guided through a process?

Why do we have a seder?

"We have a seder because it's an interesting and fun way to remember we became free." —Daniella, 11

"We commemorate the Jews leaving Egypt so we know about it, understand what they went through, and know that God who brought us out of Egypt did miracles, and we should trust Him." —Tamar, 14

"If we only told someone how good and delicious a cookie was without their even trying it, how would they really know?" —Yonah, 12

"It's a way to talk between generations, learn who we are, and impart values." —Dovie, 16

When we have a seder and follow its order, we are acknowledging God's organized arrangement and planned sequence of miracles and His loving hand in the Passover story, both in our national history as well as in our personal lives.

Why does Passover last more than one day?

Why does Passover last more than one day?

(see also page 111)

"Because we need more than one seder." —Zevi, 13

"Because the Jews had to be in the desert a long time, not just one day." —Avishai, 6

"God took time to get the Jews out of Egypt. He brought the plagues and that took time, and He did things in special ways to make it easier over time for the Jewish people to understand Him. He did it in stages. So we also need to not rush things and take our time to thank God for all that He did for us. We want Him to feel our love." —Tamar P., 6

"And this day shall be unto you for a memorial, and you shall keep it as a feast to the Lord; throughout your generations, as an ordinance forever shall you keep it as a feast. Seven days shall you eat unleavened bread."
—Exodus, Ch.12: 14-15

Why are we so careful to get rid of chametz?

**What behaviors or traits
would you like to remove from your character?**

Why are we so careful to get rid of chametz?

(see also page 112)

"In a way, chametz symbolizes slavery, because in Egypt that's what we had to eat — chametz. It's only when we were going out from Egypt that we had flat bread. Chametz is a remnant of that slavery and by not eating it on Passover, or even owning it, we own our freedom." —Avital, 15

"So we can have a pure house and make sure everything is perfect for Passover." —Tzipporah, 10

"So that by accident if you aren't so careful, you might put something chametz inside the not chametz." —Yehuda, 7

"Real redemption comes when we walk around with a candle and find this tiny trait that's holding us back from being what we could be, this little thing that's in essence ruining us—when we find it and burn it."
                    —Rabbi Shlomo Carlebach

What is a seder plate for?

Whose Passover stories would you most want to hear
at your seder? Why?

What is a seder plate for?

"To distinguish the five different symbolic foods." —Zevi, 13

"To keep things you need for the seder in front of you." —Ezra, 7

"It's to remind us of going out of Egypt." —Avishai, 6

Each item on the seder plate has special significance to the retelling of our Exodus from Egypt. Since each person must see himself or herself as having personally come out of Egypt, the seder plate helps us do that by having items on it that we see, smell, touch, and taste to viscerally experience slavery as well as our liberation.

More Of Your Questions And Reflections

More Of Your Questions And Reflections

Beginning the Seder

Which Passover ritual helps you feel most connected
to your ancestry and history?

Why do we light candles for the holiday?

In what ways do you spread light?

Why do we light candles for the holiday?

"The holiday is a special time and we show that by doing the special, holy act of lighting the candles. The candles also help us to see and to be comfortable in our homes." —Tamar, 14

"The candles make the house feel warm and cozy, peaceful, calm, and spiritual. Looking at them shining on or near the table gives us the spirit and feeling to think about how good God is all throughout the seder." —Daniella, 11

"It begins the holiday." —Miriam Shira, 9

"To symbolize that we're separating these days from regular weekdays." —Zevi, 13

"He has brought us forth from slavery to freedom, from sorrow to joy, from mourning to festivity, from darkness to great light, and from bondage to redemption." —Passover Haggadah

Why do we recline on the left when we drink wine or eat matzah?

Why do we recline on the left when we drink wine or eat matzah?

"Well, why the left? The heart is on the left and in Shema (the central prayer in Judaism where we state God's oneness) we say we'll serve God with all our heart. Maybe we're saying to God, 'I give you my heart.' We're doing it by leaning on the side of the heart and by doing it we're completing the action." —Avital, 15

"We lean because we're tired just thinking about all the work the slaves did." —Daniella, 11

"There's less chance of choking when you lean on the left." —Gila, 7

"Whenever a king tried a new food, or even ate anything, he leaned on his left side, so we're acting like kings at our seder by leaning on our left side." —Tamar C., 5

"When we lean, it's like we're saying sometimes we need other people or God to lean on, just like we did when we were slaves coming out of Egypt." —Ari, 9

"It's a way to show we've regained power and strength and freedom." —Ayelet, 9

The first Passover in Egypt was the first time since the Jews' enslavement that they were able to eat and recline and relax at their tables. Chazal, our Sages, require even the poorest Jew to recline at the seder, since this position symbolizes God bringing us out of Egypt.
—Midrash Rabbah Exodus, 20:18

Why do we wash twice: before eating the vegetable and before eating matzah?

_____

How can you experience a task you do repeatedly
as distinct and new?

Why do we wash twice:
before eating the vegetable and before eating matzah?

"At the time of the Holy Temple we all washed before eating anything moist."
—Dovie 16

"They are two different commandments. Washing before eating celery gets the children interested in the seder from the beginning because it's an unusual thing to do." —Ariel, 13

"When we wash before bread we're not just eating to eat, we're eating for spiritual reasons." —Miriam Shira, 9

"Washing is a way to be pure." —Avi, 9

"One must make changes on this night, so the children will notice and ask: 'Why is this night different?'"
 —Maimonides

Why do we dip parsley, celery, or boiled potatoes in salt water?

Who do you care for so deeply you can taste their sadness?

Why do we dip parsley, celery, or boiled potatoes in salt water?

"Parsley, celery, and boiled potato don't have much of a taste so when we dip any of them in salt water our mouths are full with the taste of the Jews' tears."
—Daniella, 11

"The parsley is green like grass that grows, which is like the Jewish people, who when they're free, grow to do good deeds." —Gila, 7

"In my family we use potatoes which are round, and go round and round, just like the Jewish people's hope that something good was going to happen. They didn't give up hope; their hope kept going round and round." —Toba, 8

"The green food is like hope and the saltwater is like sadness. So we hope the sadness goes away by dipping hope into it." —Ayelet, 9

"There weren't many crops for them to eat in Egypt so God saved them with simple food like this. What Ayelet said got me thinking. Most people's lives are filled with hope and sadness. By dipping the two together it's like we're tasting life."
—Talia, 9

"We eat parsley which is green like things in the spring and spring is life. Passover, which comes in the spring is like a new life." —Drew, 6

"After 120 years, when you will leave this world and ascend to the heavenly tribunal, you will see how meaningful and precious your tears were. You will discover that God Himself gathered them in and counted every single teardrop and treasured it like a priceless gem. And you will discover that, when some harsh and evil decree was looming over the Jewish people, one of your tears came and washed the evil away, making it null and void. Even one sincere tear is a source of salvation."
—Reb Aryeh Levin

Why do we break the middle matzah and hide away the larger half to be the afikoman?

When do you feel like you are hiding?

Why do we break the middle matzah and hide away the larger half to be the afikoman?

"We break the middle matzah because in our bodies our hearts are in the middle, and when we were slaves our hearts were broken. Now we'll go through the seder, go through everything, and at the end of the seder it will be like we're leaving Egypt, so we get the bigger part back." —Dassi, 12

"Breaking the matzah into two parts is like God giving people two paths to choose from; and we break the middle matzah because He puts us in the middle of the choices. God wants to have a little fun too; so He watches us to see where we will go. He wants us to make our own choice and to choose well." —Elana, 9

"Because we need to have a lot to eat for dessert." —Zevi, 13

"Hiding the matzah provides entertainment for the children."
—Shulchan Aruch, 473

"When two beloved friends say goodbye, some have the custom to divide a ring in half, each keeping a half to remember the love for the other. Here, too, we break the middle matzah as a way of remembering our love for God and making a covenant with Him promising to follow His ways."
—Menachem Tzion, Rabbi Mendel of Riminov

More Of Your Questions And Reflections

More Of Your Questions And Reflections

The Story . . .

What does the story of leaving Egypt
tell you about the human spirit?

Why do we say the Four Questions?

Why do we say
the Four Questions?

"Because we want children to be encouraged to ask questions. Since sometimes young children cannot think of their own questions, this gives them something to ask." —Zevi, 13

"Because it is special davening from Hashem." —Yehuda, 7

"We want to explain what Pesach is about." —Avishai, 6

"So it can remind us what we are supposed to do on Pesach." —Ezra, 7

We ask "*Ma Nishtanah ha-layla ha-zeh,*" which can be read as "What is different about tonight?" As we experience Passover and ask more than four questions, we can hope that it is we who are the what that are transformed and become different tonight.

Why is it so important to remember that we were slaves and to tell the story of leaving Egypt?

_____

What is the most significant truth or lesson of Passover
for you this year?

Why is it so important to remember that we were slaves and to tell the story of leaving Egypt?

"Forgetting is like a wall, and waiting on the other side is remembering — a passport to freedom." —Tamar, 14

"Telling stories helps us remember to make sure the same things don't happen again." —Noa, 6

"It's important to tell the story of your beginning and to remember you started with love." —Jade, 11

"If you don't remember about the time the Jews were leaving Mitzraim, then you don't remember the miracle." —Zachy, 7

"When we tell, we really learn what it means to be a Jew." —Alix, 14

"To remember you are free now to be you. When you think about times when you don't get everything you want, then you can imagine how it was for the slaves to never get anything they wanted, and to remember that time." —Davida, 9

"When we remember, we remember God, and when we talk we tell how great He is. —Tamar C., 5

"And you shall tell your son on that day, saying, 'Because of this, God did it for me when I went out of Egypt.'" —Exodus, 13:8

"Retelling the story of the Exodus reinforces our belief in God's power and ability to effect all species and individual beings—great and small."
  —Sefer HaChinuch, 21

Why did God make us slaves in the first place?

After emerging from a difficult circumstance, did you gain
understanding of why you had to go through it in the first place?

Why did God make us slaves in the first place?

"So that we would turn to God, pray to Him, cry to Him, ask for freedom, and feel closer to Him."   —Ayelet, 9

"He made us slaves so we could learn about Him, learn to respect Him, and to see his miracles. Depending on your point of view, a plague can be a miracle. Just like in the book I'm reading, 'Phantom of the Tollbooth.' In it is a bucket of water. To us it's just that, a bucket of water. To an ant, it's a wide ocean. To an elephant, it's a nice, cool drink, and to a fish it's a home. It's all about perspective. To the slaves, learning about God was a miracle."   —Talia, 9

"God wanted us to learn from being slaves. We might think being hit with a whip one time doesn't hurt so much, but it hurts a lot. We learned what it feels like to be hurt, so we know not to hurt other people."   —Ari, 9

"It was to show the Egyptians there are consequences for how they treated people. God does everything for a good reason. For us, being slaves helped us become better people, bigger, stronger, and happier in our souls."   —Elana, 9

"So that in the end we'll get to see God doing miracles for us; we just need to hang on a little longer and believe in Him."   —Daniella, 11

"Also, God was teaching us how it feels to be slaves so we don't take advantage of people."   —Avi, 9

"And you shall not oppress a stranger, for you know the feelings of the stranger, having yourselves been strangers in the land of Egypt."
—Exodus, 23:9

Why did Pharoah hate the Jews?

In what ways can we respond to hate?

Why did Pharoah hate the Jews?

"He thought the Jews were strong and rich and growing in big numbers, so Pharoah thought one day they would rule Egypt and overtake him and he didn't want to lose his land. So simply, he hated them for what he imagined they would do." —Drew, 6

"I think it bothered him to see the Jews had something inside that made them happy." —Tamar C., 5

"The Jews worshipped other things, they had different ways from the Egyptians. He hated them because they had their own way and didn't choose his way." —Elana, 9

"Just because they were Jewish was enough of a reason for Pharoah." —Noa, 6

"A new king arose over Egypt who didn't know Joseph, and he said to his people, 'Behold the people of the children of Israel are becoming more and mightier than we. We must deal wisely with them. Otherwise they may increase so much that if there is a war, they may join our enemies in fighting against us, driving us from the land.'"
—Exodus, 1:8-10

Why did Pharoah's daughter want to keep baby Moses when she found him in the river?

Is there someone or something
that you would find difficult to let go?

47

Why did Pharoah's daughter want to keep baby Moses when she found him in the river?

" 'It's only a little baby who didn't do anything wrong,' she thought, and maybe she also thought, 'What if this was me?' She put herself in his shoes." —Rose, 8

"She felt worried for a little infant and felt pity. She felt a bond with him and wanted to keep him and raise him. It was a big opportunity to save a life." —Toba, 8

"As Pharoah's daughter she probably got everything she wanted and since she had so much she wanted to do something for someone else. She had compassion for this child and was good natured. Maybe she didn't agree with her father's will and rule that the Jewish babies were to be put into the river. Since she also knew she couldn't go totally against her father, maybe she could help just this one child and this one mother. Perhaps she was also inspired by God and knew this particular baby was special." —Avital, 15

"When she [Pharoah's daughter] opened it, she saw that it was a child, a boy crying. And she had compassion on him." —Exodus 2:6

"Rabbi Jose b. Hanina said: This is because she saw that the Divine Presence was with him." —Midrash Rabba, Exodus, 1:24

Did the slaves speak Hebrew to one another?

With whom do you speak the same language?

Did the slaves speak Hebrew to one another?

"Yes, it was a way to keep themselves feeling Jewish."   —Jade, 11

"They probably did, like secrets to each other, so Pharoah wouldn't know what they were thinking."   —Miriam Shira, 9

"Only Hebrew. Back then there was no English. Maybe a little Yiddish."   —Alix, 14

"Of course."   —Zevi, 13

"No, because they were in Egypt and they didn't want to get in trouble." —Avishai, 6

Our Sages say that while in Egypt, the Jewish people held onto their identities by not changing their Hebrew names, giving Hebrew names to their children, continuing to speak Hebrew, pledging to be kind to each other, and remaining highly moral and loyal to one another.

How did the Burning Bush, from which God spoke to Moses, get on fire?

When have you experienced the miraculous?

How did the Burning Bush, from which God spoke to Moses, get on fire?

"God did it to catch Moses' attention, and He can do anything; maybe God was making a barbecue and was making it near the bush."   —Daniella, 11

"God is so holy the land couldn't take it so it set itself on fire."   —Tzipporah, 10

"God's heart is on fire and His love for Moses and the Jewish people is so great that just by turning His face towards the bush, His heart set the heart of the bush on fire."
—Tamar, 14

Rabbi Shlomo Carlebach asks, "Do you understand that you are a miracle, that your life is all miracles, that everything is a miracle? If you're living on that level where miracles are part of your life, if your trust in God reaches the level of miracle, then miracles happen to you."

Why did Moses say to God, "Who am I?" when he was chosen to go to Pharoah and lead the Jewish people out of Egypt?

What prompts you to ask yourself, "Who am I?"
How can your answer to that question be used for the good of the world?

Why did Moses say to God, "Who am I?" when he was chosen to go to Pharoah and lead the Jewish people out of Egypt?

(see also page 113)

"Who am I so special that God is talking to me? It's almost thinking out loud, 'Who am I?' Just as if you stood before a bush and God spoke to you; imagine the surprise of it." —Avital, 15

"He didn't think he was important. He probably thought, 'Who am I to do this important job? I don't speak right.'" —Talia, 9

"Right Talia, and he probably thought, 'I didn't even grow up in a Jewish home.'" —Rose, 8

"And he must have said to himself, 'I'm no better than the next guy.'" —Alix, 14

"Who expects to talk to God and talk to a powerful king?" —Avigayil, 8

"The most important thing is to give up who you are for who you might become."
—Rabbi Nachman of Bratslav

What made Moses so great?

How do you define greatness?

What made Moses so great?

(see also page 114)

"Everybody has their own thing inside them that makes them special. What made Moses special is that he really, really believed in God and was the kind of person who would do something to save the Jewish people."   —Avigayil, 8

"He has the ability to talk to God and the ability to express that He cared so much about the Jewish people and wanted the best for them. In the Torah, we see him asking for forgiveness for them many times. He had their best interests at heart, wanted their suffering to be less, and had great desire for them to succeed. He was connected to the people and loved them. A great leader has to have a connection and love what they lead."   —Avital, 15

"He was humble and he fulfilled his whole purpose in life—not everyone does that."
—Yonah, 12

"As a shepherd he followed his sheep into the desert making sure none went astray, caring for each one. This showed the kind of leader he would be, caring for each and every person."   —Dovie, 16

"He didn't obey Pharoah."   —Drew, 6

"He could have stayed in Pharoah's palace being a prince, but instead he came out to see how everyone was doing. When he saw the Jews getting hurt he helped them. He didn't have to do that."   —Tzipporah, 10

"He followed the ways of God."   —Yitzy, 6

"What makes anyone great? Essentially the answer lies in reaching and fulfilling one's potential. Moses' humility combined with his singular focus on truth and compassion stand out as his exceptional traits. He was given these traits by God, but it was he who chose to use them and maximize his potential—refining and refining himself, almost to perfection—that made him so great. All of us can do that. There's a story about Reb Zusha who said, 'When I die, I am not afraid that God will ask me, Why were you not Moses our teacher? I am afraid he will ask me, 'Why were you not Reb Zusha?'"   —Rabbi Yamin Goldsmith

When a Jewish person wanted water and all the water in Egypt had turned into blood, did they have any?

When has God performed a miracle for you?

When a Jewish person wanted water and all the water in Egypt had turned into blood, did they have any?

(see also page 115)

"The Jews had water because they didn't do anything wrong and God was taking care of them." —Gila, 7

"Yes, I agree with Gila, even if they had the same glass or pitcher the Egyptians would get blood and the Jews would get water." —Yitzy, 6

"And you shall take this staff in your hand with which you shall perform the signs."
—Exodus, 4:17

"And I will exhibit wonders in heaven and on earth."
—Joel, 2:30

How does God do miracles?

What is something mysterious and unexplainable that
has happened to you since last Passover?

How does God do miracles?

"With his Yad Chazaka, his strong hand." —Zevi, 13

"With his power." —Yehuda, 7

"He's Hashem. He can do anything." —Avishai, 6

"He is king of the world and He wants His people to survive and learn the ways to be good in the world." —Tamar P., 6

"Your right Hand O Lord, glorious in power, Your right hand, O Lord, smashes the enemy/And in the greatness of Your excellency You have overthrown them that rose up against You/ And with the blast of Your nostrils the waters piled up/ You did blow with Your wind, the sea covered them/ Who is like You among the mighty, O Lord? Who is like You, glorious in holiness too awesome for praise, doing wonders?/ You have led in Your love the people You have redeemed/ The Lord shall reign forever and ever." —Exodus, 15:6-8, 10-11, 13, 18

Why is a bit of wine removed from our cups when we read the list of punishments that the Egyptians received?

_____

When has your joy been decreased because of compassion
for another's circumstance?

Why is a bit of wine removed from our cups when we read the list of punishments that the Egyptians received?

"It's like having your finger hurt, for real, when someone else's does."
—Tamar C., 5

"We don't want to get hurt, but we don't want to hurt other people either, and we're sad that other people died. Even though they weren't nice to us, we're still sad about what happened to them, so we take a little of our wine away."
—Ezra, 7

"When we take wine from our cups we are showing that we aren't happy at another's downfall, even for those who wished ours. As we learn, at the conclusion of the Red Sea, the angels wanted to sing hymns and be joyful about the Jewish people's liberation. God held them back and said, 'My creatures are drowning and you want to sing?'"   —Talmud, Megillah, 10b

"It is of interest that in regard to the other festivals, the Torah prescribes simcha (joy). It is only in regard to Passover that this word is omitted, because although we do celebrate our independence, we cannot have a full measure of joy with the knowledge that our triumph was accompanied by the distress of the Egyptians, even though they were our sworn enemies."
     —Rabbi Abraham Twerski, MD

"Loving God, You who are full of compassion, teach me to be like You. Teach me to be kind and generous and loving, just as You are kind and generous and loving to all Your creations. Please help me develop true sensitivity, and genuine compassion toward everything in Creation."
     —Rabbi Nachman of Bratslav

Why did the Jews put blood on their doorposts before the last plague brought death to the Egyptians' firstborn?

When have you been courageous?

Why did the Jews put blood on their doorposts before the last plague brought death to the Egyptians' firstborn?

(see also page 116)

"Sheep were the Egyptians' God. Taking its blood to put on our door was brave because that's what the Egyptians worshipped. We showed respect to our God and did what He told us to do." —Rose, 8

"The angel who passed over every house would see the blood on the door and know it was a Jewish home and know to pass over it. That's why the holiday is called Passover." —Amram, 7

"For the Jews it may have represented the blood of the Egyptians. Over many years the Jews were slaves and were hurt by them, now it was their time to be hurt and to lose their blood." —Ariel, 13

"And the blood shall be to you a token upon the house where you are; and when I see the blood, I will pass over you, and there shall be no plague upon you to destroy you, when I smite the land of Egypt." —Exodus, 12:13

We sing "Dayenu" which means "it would have been enough." Would it really have been enough if God did only one thing?

Have you ever done what seemed a small act of kindness
yet it impacted deeply upon another?

**We sing "Dayenu"
which means "it would have been enough."
Would it really have been enough
if God did only one thing?**

(see also page 117)

"I don't really think one thing could have been enough because how could we be His people if we didn't have His Torah? We depended on God for each miracle."
—Toba, 8

"We don't really understand God's nature, but it is so big and so deep, if He decided to do only one thing that one thing would have been filled with His nature; so it would have been enough." —Tamar, 14

"No, we needed everything God did and we still need everything He does."
—Amram, 7

"Therefore, how much more so do we owe abundant thanks to God for all the manifold good He bestows on us. He brought us out of Egypt, He executed judgement upon the Egyptians and their gods. He slew their firstborn. He gave to us their wealth. He split the sea for us, led us through it on dry land and drowned our oppressors in it. He provided for our needs for forty years and fed us the Manna. He gave us Shabbat, led us to Mount Sinai and gave us the Torah. He brought us into the Land of Israel and built for us the Temple to atone for all our mistakes."
—Passover Haggadah

Why is the Yam Suf (the sea that split) which is dark green and dark blue mixed together, called the Red Sea?

Why is the Yam Suf (the sea that split) which is dark green and dark blue mixed together, called the Red Sea?

"When the Jews went through the water they probably had cuts that were bleeding from all their hard work and it turned the sea red, so they called it the Red Sea."
—Rose, 8

"A mapmaker copied it wrong from another map. It was originally called the Reed Sea. By mistake he wrote the Red Sea. Then other people kept copying from him."
—Dassi, 12

"It's called the Red Sea because it's like a red mark on a map marking an important spot." —Avi, 9

"Or maybe Avi, it's the things the Egyptians did wrong that turned the sea red."
—Ayelet, 9

"Maybe it's the Egyptians' blood." —Ari, 9

"Or maybe it's the things the Jews did wrong, like talking badly about other people. Those wrong things were represented by the color red. When the Jews went through the Yam Suf it was a transformation. They left their homes, everything they formed, and quickly rushed out to Hashem because they believed in Him. As part of their transformation the red was removed from them and went into the sea instead."
—Ariel, 13

Nachshon Ben Aminadav serves as a paradigm of courage and faith, inspiring others to follow in his footsteps, as he seized the initiative to plunge into the Red Sea when the Jews were being pursued by the Egyptians. He believed God would intervene on behalf of the Jewish people. Our Sages say the waters engulfed his body to his nostrils; still he continued. Then, and only then, did the waters split.

How did the Jewish people know which way to go when they left Egypt?

What can you learn about a way of being from our wandering in the desert?

How did the Jewish people know which way to go when they left Egypt?

"They didn't know which way to go, but they went anyway because they believed in God and He showed them the way." —Ariel, 13

When the sea opened, everyone knew it was a miracle, and they knew they should go through and follow the miracle." —Zachy, 7

"Clouds protected them all around and led them." —Rose, 8

"At night a pillar of fire floating in the air gave them light to know which way to go." —Gila, 7

"God gave Moses directions, kind of like Mapquest." —Avigayil, 8

"Anywhere you've been enslaved, you have a dream to live in freedom. You always wait and imagine it, so you listen carefully to those around you to know and learn about the surrounding area to get an understanding of what your escape plan could be." —Avital, 15

"May it be your will, Lord our God and God of our ancestors, to lead us in peace and direct our steps in peace. May you bring us to our destination in life, happiness, and peace. Deliver us from the hand of every enemy or danger on the road. May we obtain favor, kindness, and compassion in Your eyes and in the eyes of all we meet. Hear the voice of our supplication, because You, God, hear prayers and supplications. Blessed are You God who hears prayers." —Prayer for a Safe Journey

Why did God take us out of Egypt?

**What can you take out from the Exodus story to bring about
redemption for yourself, your relationships,
the Jewish community, and the greater world?**

Why did God take us out of Egypt?

"We were still alive and whenever you're alive you're here for a reason, you have a purpose. He took us out to live out our reasons." —Ari, 9

"The Jewish people saw Moses as a role model and they saw him praying to God, so they started to pray, too. God took their prayers and listened to them saying they wanted to leave Egypt. He saw the good in us and in our hearts; we all have a piece of Him in our hearts and souls. He loved us and took us out." —Rose, 8

"He took us out so we could show the whole world how to be nice, good people."
—Miriam Shira, 9

"So we could be free and learn the Torah and we learn the Torah so we can learn about God, about all the history that came before us, and about the miracles in the world." —Daniella, 11

"God made a promise to Abraham that one day the Jewish people would be brought to a land flowing with milk and honey. If He didn't take us out of Egypt, He would have broken His promise, and God doesn't break promises." —Yonah, 12

"So that we could be His nation. He already chose us to be His nation, but in Egypt it was hard for us to act like His nation because we couldn't obey the mitzvot, commandments, so much." —Tamar, 14

"To marry us." —Amram, 7

"He tooks us out because He knew our hearts and He knew we are spiritual like Him." —Avigayil, 8

"I am my Beloved's and my Beloved is mine." —Song of Songs, 6:3

What does it really mean to be free?

_____

When have you felt free?

What does it really mean to be free?

"Freedom is knowing what's possible." —Daniella, 11

"And Daniella, believing in God helps make the possible happen." —Tamar, 14

"The power of choosing." —Zevi, 13

"When you're not a slave and when you get to have a family and stuff like that."
—Yehuda, 7

"You can call your own shots and you can of course choose to listen to the Torah."
—Tamar P., 6

"Real freedom is that noble spirit by which the individual and indeed the whole people are elevated to become loyal to their inner essential self, to the image of God within them."
—Rav Avraham Yitzchak Kook

More Of Your Questions And Reflections

More Of Your Questions And Reflections

The Meal

What personal blessing can you give to each person at your seder table?

Why do we need to eat matzah?

Why do we need to eat matzah?

"By eating plain, flat matzah instead of fluffy bread we learn to not be puffed up big shots."   —Yitzy, 6

"They didn't have time for the bread to rise because they were in such a hurry to be free. They had to grab the moment, take the moment and go. If we want to do something, no matter how hard it is, we have to go for it. We took our matzah and reached for the stars."   —Toba, 8

"Matzah is also called "lechem oni," poor man's bread. Poor people, like the slaves, can't afford nice bread so we eat matzah to remember what it was like when we couldn't afford anything."   —Ari, 9

"When Pharoah had us working we felt like we were crumbling, and matzah crumbles."   —Drew, 6

"We eat it because it's a commandment of the Torah to eat it, and also because it commemorates the Passover sacrifice or offering that was eaten that first seder night and that was brought to the Temple in Temple times."   —Dovie, 16

"This was a big day, leaving Egypt, and every part of our history is important. We're supposed to remember every single important moment that happend, so we copy what they did and eat what they ate."   —Elana, 9

"On the first day, on the 14th of the month, in the evening you shall eat matzah."
—Exodus, 12:18

Why do we say a blessing thanking God for the commandment to eat bitter herbs?

Do you believe things happen to you for your own good, even when they are difficult?

Why do we say a blessing thanking God for the commandment to eat bitter herbs?

"I wonder what the bitter herbs would say if they could talk."   —Yonah, 12

"Probably they would have an inferiority complex."   —Jade, 11

"No I don't think so. I think they would say, 'We're important because we're like medicine that tastes yucky but does good things for you.' "   —Tzipporah, 10

"Also, when you taste something that's bitter, then you really, really appreciate the sweet things."   —Yonah, 12

"Kind of like going to a place that's air-conditioned on a 100 degree day, or a cold drink when you're really thirsty.   —Noa, 6

"Or hope when you've been hopeless."   —Alix, 14

"Even in the beginning when we don't know something is for our own good, in the end it always is. I think that's why we say a blessing when we eat bitter herbs."   —Dassi, 12

There is an anecdote told of Rabbi Pinchas HaLevi Horowitz: He asked his Rebbe, Rabbi Dov Ber how the Torah expects one to "Bless God for the bad the same way as he blesses Him for the good" (Mishnah Berachot, 9:5). Rabbi Dov Ber directed him to Reb Zusha. Reb Zusha who lived in abject poverty and suffered many tribulations answered Rabbi Pinchas' question in the following way: "I have never experienced anything bad in my life! Everything God did for me was good, even if it seemed the opposite."

Why do we eat a sandwich of matzah and maror (bitter herbs)?

Why do we eat a sandwich of matzah and maror (bitter herbs)?

(see also page 118)

"We eat it now because being slaves back then they didn't have time for sandwiches." —Noa, 6

"It's a sandwich of sadness and happiness. The matzah is happiness because we were becoming free, and the maror is sadness because it's bitter. We eat it together to remember the whole story." —Drew, 6

"Because that's what Hillel did and he was a very respected rabbi." —Zevi, 13

"Because when the story took place that's what the Jews did." —Yehuda, 7

"To remember their bitter lives." —Tamar P., 6

"To remind us of the Temple, we do as Hillel did in Temple times, combining matzah and maror in a sandwich, eating them together, fulfilling what is written in the Torah: 'They shall eat it with matzahs and bitter herbs'."
—Passover Haggadah

How can we make
the seder meal special?

What is your recipe for creating fullness in your life?

How can we make
the seder meal special?

(see also page 120)

"By enjoying the food." —Zevi, 13

"Help cook it." —Yehuda, 7

"By singing, smiling, and being nice to other people who are around you."
—Ezra, 7

"Give brachot (blessings) to people that you love at your seder." —Avishai, 6

*"Share special time with family that you have invited and daven (pray) together
extra hard thanking Hashem for the things He did for us."* —Tamar P., 6

The seder is a journey. Just as when we travel we take what is needed for the
trip and our arrival in a new place, so here too we gather together the essential,
especially the people we love.

Why is it so important to look for the afikoman?

What do you seek?

Why is it so important to look for the afikoman?

"Every half wants its other piece." —Avigayil, 8

"It's like the Jewish people leaving Egypt and looking for their home. We're acting like them by becoming "lookers" looking for the afikoman. We're trying to find the afikoman's way home and our way home." —Yona, 8

"And looking for and finding the afikoman is like putting two things together that were separated. Bringing them together is like making peace and finding sweet freedom." —Talia, 9

"It's something kids can look forward to and it helps them to stay up." —Rose, 8

"We can't finish the seder without it." —Dovie, 16

"When something important to us is hidden, we want to look for it with the hope we'll find it." —Drew, 6

"When we find what has been hiding we love it like it's new." —Ayelet, 9

This step in the seder, which is especially focused on the children, is called Tzafun, which means hidden. Maybe we too can seek what is hidden. Just as children search for the afikoman with wide-eyed anticipation and a certainty that it will be found, we as well can trust that at some point we will find that which we seek.
—Rabbi Yamin Goldsmith

Why is the afikoman the last thing we are to taste?

What do you want to savor and be left with
from your seder experience?

Why is the afikoman the last thing we are to taste?

"We want to end with the simple food the slaves ate. To really feel what Passover is about we want to keep the taste of matzah in our mouths." —Elana, 9

"I think we don't finish the seder without it because the afikoman is the point of the meal. By eating the afikoman last it's like we're asking for the most important point: for a good life, for chances, and to be left with the taste of getting close to God." —Ayelet, 9

"Afikoman is the hope of the Jewish people, of a new beginning, of greatness. We want to keep and hold on to the taste of the hope that each day is a new chance to reach for greatness." —Tamar, 14

"The afikoman represents hope and in the end, we all want to have hope." —Ari, 9

"It's dessert." —Avi, 9

"When we were slaves we worked for just a little food, just a little reward, and we were grateful for it. Now the children work to find the afikoman, and when they finally find the good thing they were looking for, we eat it last and are reminded of the reward. By being left with the taste of matzah, it helps us remember to not take the little things for granted." —Ariel, 13

"You may want to settle on something not so heavy, not so filling, to end the meal. One of the last things we did in Egypt was to make matzah, so we celebrate that and their leaving by eating it last." —Talia, 9

On Passover, the middle matzah, that is to become the afikoman, begins whole. During the seder this matzah is broken, reflecting our brokenness, or lack of wholeness. We eat the half that is not the afikoman. The process of the seder is the movement from wholeness to brokenness, to wholeness again, this time internalized. How? By eating the afikoman we are uniting the broken matzah within ourselves. We are creating completion inside, reflecting the movement of the seder, the movement of the Jewish people, the movement of our personal lives from shattered to *shleimut*, to a wholeness which is peace.

Why do we also say a blessing after the meal?

The Hebrew word for blessing is *bracha,*
which sounds like *braicha,* the Hebrew word for a spring.
How is a blessing like a free-flowing spring of water?

Why do we also say a blessing after the meal?

"How can it possibly be right to take something, anything, without saying, 'Thank you?' The Torah understands that, and teaches us to thank God after we eat a meal; He gives us everything. Giving back with blessings is like saying there's a ladder connecting heaven and earth." —Daniella, 11

"To thank Hashem that we're not hungry anymore." —Tamar P., 6

"To thank Hashem for the food He gave us. Some people don't have food and we thank Him that we're not like that." —Avishai, 6

"For everything, Lord our God, we give thanks to you, may Your name be blessed forever by all, as it is written, 'When you have eaten and been satisfied, you will bless the Lord Your God.'"
—Birkat HaMazon, the Grace After Meals

More Of Your Questions And Reflections

More Of Your Questions And Reflections

Moving Toward Completion

When have you felt redeemed?

Why do we need to open the door for Elijah? Can't he just come in?

How are you changed as a person
by the act of opening a door?

Why do we need to open the door for Elijah?
Can't he just come in?

"Just because you're invisible doesn't mean you can just walk in." —Ezra, 7

"To welcome him in." —Tamar P., 6

"It's out of respect for him. Opening the door is showing him respect. That way he doesn't have to just walk in." —Toba, 8

"He could just come in, but he's special and we want to show him we know that."
—Tamar C., 5

"We err if we believe that Elijah the Prophet, comes through the door. Rather, he must enter through our hearts and souls."
      —The Kotzker Rebbe

"The concern of Judaism is primarily not how to find the presence of God in the world of things but how to let Him enter the ways in which we deal with things."
      —Rabbi Abraham Joshua Heschel

Who is Elijah and why do we leave out wine for him?

_____

If you could ask Elijah one question, what would it be?

Who is Elijah and why do we leave out wine for him?

"Elijah brings the message that the time of the Messiah, the time of total redemption and peace has come. When we welcome him with wine we're telling him we want him to come now with his message." —Yona, 8

"I'm thinking he probably likes wine better than beer." —Yitzy, 6

"The Haggadah says, 'Anyone who is hungry, let him come and eat.' It's a special act of goodness to do this. The same way we welcome a guest and want them to feel comfortable, we also want to welcome Elijah and share with him." —Tamar, 14

"We put out wine for him because we're showing we don't just wait for a miracle to happen to us. We're not lazy and we're willing to help God make good things happen." —Ariel, 13

"It's a spiritual thing, like when we welcome in Shabbat. We don't want to be casual like, 'Oh, hey Eliyahu, you're here.' We want him to feel greeted." —Elana, 9

Elijah, the much loved prophet, known in Hebrew as Eliyahu HaNavi, is mentioned as the one to usher in the time of redemption, bringing peace and healing to a broken world. When he comes, he will also resolve unanswered questions of law and practice, including whether we drink a fifth cup of wine at the seder, the cup we now reserve for him, for the fifth expression of redemption, "and I will bring you into the land." We believe Elijah comes on Passover and visits every seder.

Why can't we see Elijah?

Despite not being able to see God,
when have you sensed His presence?

Why can't we see Elijah?

"He was humble and just wants to go in and do his job and be modest about it. He didn't want to be seen so much; maybe even, that's why he takes little sips."
—Talia, 9

"It's not the right time yet for us to see him and we have to wait for the right opportunity. We're waiting for the perfect moment for him to tell us the final redemption is coming."   —Miriam Shira, 9

"We can't see Elijah because he's already in heaven and when he comes to visit us he's wearing heaven's clothes, which are too sparkly for human eyes to see."
—Tamar C., 5

"So maybe we'll learn from this to know people for what they do and not by how they look."   —Jade, 11

"When we were slaves we weren't free physically and we couldn't see properly because we also weren't free emotionally and spiritually; and still we're not. The Jewish people wanted their lives to be better, so we learn from them that we should work for that too, and free our minds emotionally and spiritually so we can be free enough to really see."   —Ariel, 13

"He's a spirit and an angel and God probably doesn't want us to see him. We trust in our hearts he's there."   —Avigayil, 8

Is the only way to see with your eyes? Look at the salt water on your table. Maybe you even poured the salt into the water to help get ready for the seder; so you know it's there, but it is invisible. We taste the salt when we dip the vegetable into the water, or if we were to pour it over an open wound we would feel it sting.

We can use all five of our senses to know something, but maybe there is another way to "see," with yet another sense, one that senses. Some people call it a feeling, perhaps a gut feeling, or an intuition: a knowing that is beyond the usual way of understanding. In the book, *The Little Prince,* it is said, "Here is my secret. It is very simple. One sees clearly only with the heart. Anything essential is invisible to the eyes."

Why can't we see Elijah? That depends; in what ways do you see?

Since God is already complete and He knows everything in our hearts, why is a big part of the seder our singing songs of praise to Him?

When have you been so grateful that saying "Thank you"
feels like arriving empty-handed?

Since God is already complete and He knows everything in our hearts, why is a big part of the seder our singing songs of praise to Him?

"We thank Hashem because He is always making miracles. He made lots of miracles when we were slaves to make us free and He's still going to make a big, big one . . . Moshiach!" —Zachy, 7

"Hashem always does miracles. Some are obvious, like when that plane crash-landed in the Hudson River and everyone survived, and some are hidden miracles that we can't quite see everyday. But every day we're alive is a miracle, so we thank Him." —Davida, 9

"Because it's respectful to compliment a king." —Zevi, 13

"Because He is the ruler of the world." —Yehuda, 7

"To thank Him for really paying attention to us and watching over us." —Tamar P., 7

"Were our mouth as full of song as the sea, and our tongues full of joyous song as the multitude of waves, and our lips as full of prayers as the wide expanse of the heavens, and our eyes as radiant as the sun and the moon; our hands outspread like eagles of heaven and our feet swift as deer . . . we still could not thank you sufficiently."
—Nishmat prayer

Why do we say
"Next year in Jerusalem"
at the end of the seder?

Where do you long to be? Why?

Why do we say "Next year in Jerusalem" at the end of the seder?

(see also page 121)

"We want the time of the Messiah to come and when the Messiah comes we'll be in Jerusalem. We want to be in Israel; it's holy land. What we really should be saying is next day or next minute in Jerusalem, since we want it to be sooner than next year." —Toba, 8

"We say that because we want to be in Israel next year; but I have a question for you. Why do people say, 'Next year in Jerusalem' if you are already in Israel. Oh wait, I know why. Maybe because if you're there, you don't know if things are going to change, and you hope next year you'll still be there." —Yitzy, 6

"And Yitzy, Jerusalem isn't just a place on the earth, it's also a place in your mind and your heart." —Amram, 7

"Wherever I go, I go to Jerusalem."
—Rabbi Nachman of Bratslav

More Of Your Questions And Reflections

More Of Your Questions And Reflections

Further Reflections

What hopes do you have for the coming year?

Why does Passover last more than one day?

Dear Children,

When is your birthday?

Have you ever excitedly waited for it to come? Did you note the ¼, ½, and ¾ marks in the year until it was so close you started counting down the days until it arrived? Have you helped prepare for it and plan the celebration?

If you have, then you know the feeling when you wake up on the morning of that special day. It's new like a beginning, yet familiar and safe because you're surrounded by love. You receive thoughtful gifts, eat a special dessert and feel blessed; and then it's over. Don't you wish it could last just a little bit more?

Passover is the birthday of the Jews becoming a nation and we celebrate it for more than one day because the Torah teaches us it lasts for seven days. (It became the custom to add an extra day outside the land of Israel.)

God planned and prepared a beautiful festival, and being the best party planner, He knew one day just wasn't enough.

Whenever your special day is, including seder night, "Happy Birthday!"

Love,
Sharon

Why are we so careful to get rid of chametz?

During the year, if a tiny piece of unkosher food falls into a pot of kosher food, it is still considered kosher if the ratio of kosher to non-kosher is 60:1; but on Passover, if even the slightest speck of *chametz*, leavened food, intermingles with Passover food it is considered unkosher for Passover. Not only can't we eat any leavened product during Passover, we can't even own it. The tiniest bit of *chametz* changes everything.

Have you ever had a splinter in your foot? If you have, then you know that even if it is a tiny splinter, every step you take hurts. Probably, you even walk a little funny, not in your usual way. You need to take the splinter out because it doesn't belong there. It's not part of the natural you. In fact, if you don't take it out it can become infected and possibly make the rest of your body sick.

It is our job to be very careful to remove that which doesn't belong, not leaving a sixtieth or even a millionth of it inside ourselves. That way, we can once again be our pure, essential selves and become free from the things impeding us from how we really want to walk. On Passover, that's what *chametz* is; it's a splinter and it must come out, so that we are free to be all of who it is possible for us to be.

Why did Moses say to God, "Who am I?" when he was chosen to go to Paroah and lead the Jewish people out of Egypt?

Passover is a holiday for searching. Before its arrival we look for *chametz* and rid ourselves of it in order to be ready for the holiday. We ask the Ma Nishtanah, the Four Questions, and pursue answers. We hide and then seek the afikoman.

When Moses asks, "Who am I?" perhaps he too is searching, studying his heart and examining himself; and for the seven days he and God spoke face to face at the Burning Bush (which historically became the seven days of Passover) he was looking for answers to that question.

Our Sages tell us Moses was the humblest of men and his questioning, "Who am I?" reflected his great modesty. It is said, as well, that it expressed his deep sensitivity toward his brother Aaron's feelings since Moses was uncomfortable playing a more significant role than his older sibling. It may also be that having grown up as an Egyptian prince, Moses wondered who he was to lead the Jewish people out of Egypt when he himself never directly experienced what they had. There for a week, at the bush that was burning but not consumed, Moses saw the miraculous, and came to know he could live in the possibility of doing the impossible, to do a job that seemed beyond the do-able.

He just needed to prepare by thinking carefully about himself, searching and gathering up every ounce of who he was in order to step into who he was to become. The Torah tells us that when Moses arrived at the Burning Bush, God called out, "Moses, Moses." He responded, "Hineni"— here am I. God commanded him to go back to the Jewish people and tell them, "Eh-yeh Imach" — I will be with you, I am with the people now and I shall be with them in the future.

There is a beautiful parable known by many as *Footprints*. In it, a man dreams he is walking along the beach with God. Scenes from his life pass before him. For most of his life he notices two sets of footprints in the sand, his and God's. During the more difficult times though, he sees only one set. "God," he asks, "why weren't You walking with me when I needed You most?" God answers, "I love you and would never leave you. It was at those times that I carried you."

When you find yourself in a situation that calls out to you, yet seems impossible, search yourself and ask, "Who am I?" and take every bit of your goodness, abilities, strengths, and potential, and believe it's possible to come through challenges without being consumed. Then, with your whole and complete heart say, "Hineni." I am ready now to participate in creating miracles. It is then, Eh-yeh will be with you and you are not walking alone.

What made Moses so great?

The following story about the greatness of Moses' character is found in the Mishnah commentary *Tiferet Yisrael*.

When Moses brought the Jews out of Egypt, all the nations heard and trembled. They wondered greatly about this man, Moses, who by his hand so many miracles were wrought. Therefore, one Arabian king decided to send his royal artist to portray Moses' image and bring it to him. When he brought back the picture, the king gathered all the occult scholars of the realm. He asked them to analyze the physiognomy before them and reconstruct all his character traits for the purpose of discerning from where his power is derived.

They came as a group before the king and said, "If we were to report on this famous man as portrayed in this painting, we would have to declare that this is an extraordinarily evil individual. His traits include vanity, avarice, cold-heartedness, in short all the negative traits in the world."

The king exploded, "How can this be? Haven't I heard from every source available the exact opposite of this?" The gathered scholars trembled. An argument broke out between the artist and the scholars each claiming the incompetence of the other. The king who burned to know the truth, traveled to the camp of Israel in the desert. He went with cavalry and chariots, and entered the camp. Upon his entry he saw Moses, the man of God, and rushed up to him pulling out the picture as he went; and he looked exactly as portrayed in the drawing. His heart felt faint and he was overwhelmed by doubts. He approached Moses, bowed before him, and related all that had transpired. He said, "At first I thought the artist missed the true image, but now I see he hit the mark, so it must be my scholars have failed me."

Moses, the man of God responded, "No, both your painters and your scholars are wonderful in their abilities. You should know, if I were like my true nature as was described to you, I'd be as useful as dry wood. I am not embarrassed to tell you that all the shortcomings and failings which were judged within me are all connected to my nature, and perhaps even more than they surmised. And I, with great strength, have combated and defeated them, until I have acquired for myself an opposite, second nature. It's for this reason I am respected both in heaven above and earth below."

—Rabbi Yisrael Lipshitz

When a Jewish person wanted water and all the water in Egypt had turned into blood, did they have any?

In the Torah, the plagues are most often called, not punishments, but *otot*, signs. What's the first thing that comes to mind for you when you hear the word signs? For me, it's signs along the road.

EXIT COMING-THE ROAD SPLITS-CHILDREN AT PLAY

They are guideposts letting us know what is up ahead, written by those who have a bigger picture. They're meant for our good and are there to protect all of us. Imagine being on a road without signs. It's a bit like being in school and not knowing the schedule of the day, having no idea what comes next. It's certainly a feeling of not being "in the know."

Even though it seemed as if God was not taking care of our needs during the period when we were slaves, when the plagues came, God's involvement in our lives became apparent and revealed. His all-encompassing Presence which had seemed hidden became known. Miracles were out in the open.

The plagues are also called *moftim*, wonders. The world, even today, is full of *otot* and *moftim*. It is easy to not notice the signs and wonders in the world. Sometimes we do notice but we question if they are true, since they usually aren't something we can touch and typically don't follow the rules we most often use to interpret our world. The first step is to believe they are there and to believe they are real. Sometimes they come as a dream, sometimes as a "coincidence," and sometimes as a knowing deep inside ourselves beyond our conscious information bank. When we do read them, they are like a mirror positioned at a sharp bend in the road enabling us to see what is normally hidden from view. The signs are God's way of calling out to us, "My precious one, I'm taking care of you. I know what you need. Here is a message from Me."

So yes, the Jewish people's needs were visibly cared for when water was turned into blood during the first plague. They did have water. Even if an Egyptian shared a glass with a Jew, the Egyptian had blood and the Jew had water. But the Jews had far more than water, since now they were "in the know" and had understanding. We can be as they were when we realize that our road is paved with signs and wonders by the One who creates them and Who has the biggest picture.

Why did the Jews put blood on their doorposts before the last plague brought death to the Egyptians' firstborn?

Before the arrival of the final plague, the Jewish people were prepared for it by being asked to put the blood of a sheep on their doorpost. In this way, God would know which houses to pass over. How is it that God, who knows everything, needed a sign to know which houses to skip? Obviously He didn't; so for whom do you think the blood was put there?

The Egyptians worshipped sheep. By taking the life of this specific creature, a god to them, we were saying, "We don't worship what you worship. Your god is not our God. We can now stand up to you and not be afraid to believe in what we know to be true."

The Hebrew word for sacrifice is *korban* which means to draw close. In making this sacrifice we were able to come closer to God, to what is real. In fact, there is an opinion that the blood was put inside the door so that as the Jews sat in their homes eating a dinner of roasted lamb, it was they who were looking at the blood of a sheep. Can you transport yourself back in time and feel the power of that moment? They were dedicating themselves to God, to a novel world view, and to a new way of living, and the blood was standing witness to this profound moment of transformation.

It takes courage to act and think differently from those around you. It is not easy to separate yourself from the values of the surrounding people and culture. Maybe in your world certain types of sneakers or clothing with particular labels are considered important to have; or maybe your group of friends adopts a negative opinion about a person or group of people labeling them, without each deciding for themselves.

That night in Egypt, the Jews laid down a path we can revisit and make our own. In their staring at the blood on their doorposts, it is as if they were saying, "We've taken from the herd, but we're not thinking with herd mentality. We have a new way of being and a way to draw closer to the truth and to that which we value."

**We sing "Dayenu" at the seder which means
"it would have been enough."
Would it really have been enough if God did only one thing?**

A Stack of 15 Gifts, Unwrapped

15 steps of the seder
15 steps up to the Beit HaMikdash*
15 times we say, "Dayenu"
for God's 15 presents
stacked one on another
like a staircase to heaven
each part already complete
given with a whole heart
from One who harnesses His Love
from the bottom of His replenishing Heart
a *chag** of giving and receiving
a circle of return
the beginning in the end

And the end being in the beginning
we tell the good, Hakarat HaTov
15 ways, "Dayenu"
for every detail of every gift
like the painting you made for Mom
her saying so much more than, "It's beautiful"
she tells you and everyone out loud
"I love your brushstrokes,
and the way you put in the sky,
and how it flows inside-out
from an opening in your blue un-red heart"
And in the noticing, nothing is little
about the steps

We're thankful
even to say, "Todah"*
allowing us to love the gift
to delight in and love the Giver more
and so we know we need no more, to step
into the white of the clouds
to step into the sky blue
to step into the Arms of the One, without end, Above
who climbs into you
and your just emptied-just filled heart
till tears just aren't enough
and on His shoulder, in embrace
you cry, unwrapped
"Dayenu"
one step
it would have been enough

*Beit HaMikdash: The Holy Temple   *chag: holiday   *Todah: Thank you

Why do we eat a sandwich of matzah and maror (bitter herbs)?

Once there lived a king, a sweet, beautiful young man, extraordinary in kindness and wisdom, Despite his young age, the people of his kingdom recognized who he was and learned how to love more deeply from his soft gentleness, profound sensitivity, and understanding of truth.

He had lived in a palace where all were welcomed and would travel great distances to visit. In gathering there, their hearts and their eyes looked anew and with greater love for one another. Stirred by the melodies surrounding them: the singing, the instruments being played, the whispers of the land itself—the place of their ancient roots—and the devotion and prayers, spoken and silent, their souls ascended. The harmony and beauty of the place itself, like their king, returned them home restored.

Sadly though, their king lived in the palace no longer, for it was destroyed. The people of the kingdom cried for the home of their hearts, for their king, and for all they had lost. Though the king could easily have chosen to live in many beautiful places, and the people of the land would build him anything he wished, he told them, "Not yet. The time isn't now, though it is coming soon."

He chose instead to dwell where his palace once stood, to honor it and the ground graced by having held it. There on palace grounds, in cold and in rain and under the hot sun, with just a lit candle nearby that had been saved from his sacred home where it had always burned, the king stayed, encircled by beautiful birds sent to shelter him and the eternal candle.

The people also remembered and visited their beloved king. He spoke words of kindness and wisdom he had taught them at the palace before, until they began sharing those words among themselves, knowing them so well they hardly needed words at all. Even how they looked at the king and at one another said they understood. With longing for the palace to be rebuilt and with hope that they could gladden their king's heart, they'd sit together and talk about old times, the celebrations they had had there, the learning they exchanged, and the special offerings of food they had brought; and together, in remembering, they wept full, uniting even further their hearts and minds.

The birds whose job it was to help the king keep the candle lit, gathered peoples' streams of tears in their wings, protecting the flame. They carried their great sadness up, up, up, way past the clouds, sending it into the sun, which split the tears into a million particles of light. Down the light then came, shaping itself before the king's eyes into his palace, a palace of light, looking just as it had when it was made of stone.

"Look," he told the people, "Because we learned to love so deeply and show extraordinary kindness to one another, the time is now. Our tears, heavy with longing, merited to enter the windows of heaven, letting us see below what was always there." In exuberant joy the people sang songs of praise and danced, faster and faster still, till they fell into the soft grass and saw the clouds dancing too. Once again, they celebrated and learned and ate special offerings of food, ethereal sandwiches of tears and light, to remember what they could now see; to remember what they would never forget.

How can we make the seder meal special?

NEED:

-at least 4 good questions
-overflowing cups of joy
-bittersweet memories
-unlimited amounts of beautiful people, can be:
        *family who are like friends
        *friends who are like family
        *any person who one day may become a friend
-no Wonder Bread, but lots of wonder
-no gossip, but lots of talk of miracles

STIR IN:

-recollections of the meal eaten by the Jewish people on their last night in Egypt, and our redemption
-praises of God's Greatness

PRESENTATION:

At the set table present it all with love, giving generously to others without expecting anything in return, provide opportunities for them to feel safe and appreciated, and hold up a mirror reflecting the best of who they are so they can embrace those strengths and grow to yet other strengths.

THE LAST STEP:

Leave room for the special, hidden away dessert and finish the meal before midnight so you eat that afikoman in time.

ENJOY!

Why do we say "Next year in Jerusalem" at the end of the seder?

Imagine going on vacation with your family to see the world, traveling from place to place. You experience many beautiful things, appreciate God's creation, and learn much. It's exciting and interesting, especially in the beginning. Imagine though, you are journeying for weeks and weeks, and after awhile you're tired of moving from one location to another without any one place to call home. You begin to long for your bed, your pillow, your favorite blanket, for the place you love and care about best of all, and where you too feel most cared for and loved.

Finally, finally, after seeing the Rocky Mountains and the Eiffel Tower, the Ivory Coast and the Costa Rican rain forest, you arrive home: the place where you are most relaxed and comfortable, where you can be yourself. What a relief! That's what Israel is for the Jewish people. It's our home.

Imagine also, the land of Israel being like a body. The body has arms and legs, a mind, and a heart. Jerusalem is the heart. We can't live without a heart. Picture further, that the heart has a heart—an innermost point—a center, from which the pulse of the heart beats. That's the Beit HaMikdash, the Holy Temple. We still have a part of it from so long ago: the Kotel, also called the Western Wall. It's the last remaining section of a retaining wall that surrounded the Temple's westernmost side. It's still standing, a witness to what was. We can go there, be ourselves, pray, and pour out our hearts at the place that's the heart of the heart.

Whether we live far away from the Kotel in America, Australia, or China, or close by in Jerusalem or Tsfat, we can remember the Beit HaMikdash and what we are missing. We are free but we aren't yet complete; and just the very thought of the heart of the heart, stirs our hearts with emotion.

After taking the fifteen steps of the seder, a journey that began with *Kiddush* on the first cup of wine, through *Nirtzah*, the mutual acceptance of the Jewish people by God and God by the Jewish people, we reach a new place where we can no longer contain ourselves or quiet our rapidly beating hearts, and we cry out for every stone of the Kotel, every plant growing in between, every cloud above. We call out from our depths, like a shofar blast, for that which we still long. "We're coming," we cry. "We're coming home. *Leshanah haba'ah b'Yerushalayim.* Next year in Jerusalem."

More Of Your Questions And Reflections

THE CONTRIBUTORS

Rabbi Leo Baeck, (1873-1956), was a German Jewish scholar and liberal, modern Jew. He wrote about having emotional awareness, experiencing the Divine, living a life committed to ethical acts and universal good, and maintaining our Jewish peoplehood.

Sharon Black has been an educator for three decades at SAR Academy in Riverdale, New York, where she created and directs a Schoolwide Enrichment Program. It is based on a broadened conception of giftedness and it offers enrichment learning opportunities to every child. Sharon founded ARTS EDJE, a teacher institute for the arts and is launching the Grand Circle, an intergenerational collaborative built around the arts. She is a published poet and author of numerous educational articles including: "Equal Opportunity Excellence For All," and "The Gifts of Seeing: Making Excellence Visible in Arts Education," and has served as editor-in-chief of *Tzaddik Magazine* and as its "Life Lessons" memoir columnist. Sharon is the author of *The Wisdom of a Starry Night, Using the Power of Great Art for Self-Awareness* (Barnes and Noble Publishing), a work that uses inquiry in tandem with art masterpieces as a tool for self-exploration.

Rabbi Shlomo Carlebach, (1925-1994), reached out to thousands of people over more than four decades of traveling to various communities. He taught the sweetness of Torah and how to pray with all your heart. Song and storytelling were his vehicles for bringing people closer to Judaism. His synagogue, in New York City, carries on his legacy.

Tamar Cohen, age 5, loves to sing, act, and learn about the stars.

Talia Cohen, age 9, is a Jewish feminist who is interested in diplomacy and promoting human rights.

Avishai Ebenstein, age 6, loves playing chess and thinking about math questions.

Rose Frankel, age 8, loves to cook and read and swim.

Rabbi Yamin Goldsmith, is well known and respected for his warm and engaging personality. He served in the Israeli Defense Forces for two years, was ordained at the Rabbi Isaac Elchanan Theological Seminary of Yeshiva University, is completing his doctoral dissertation in curriculum and teaching at Columbia University Teachers

College, and is *menahel*, principal, of Yeshivat Sha'alvim for Women in Jerusalem.

Rabbi Abraham Joshua Heschel, (1907-1972), a descendent of two important Hasidic dynasties, was born in Warsaw. He was a significant and revered Jewish theologian. After obtaining rabbinical ordination he acquired a doctorate. He escaped the Nazis and found his way to the United States where he was a Professor of Jewish Ethics and Mysticism for twenty-seven years at Jewish Theological Seminary of America. He had a special interest in the prophets, social action, spirituality, the mystery of being, and the proper way for Jews to incorporate religion into their lives.

Avi Hirschfield, age 9

Dassi Hirschfield, age 12

Rabbi Abraham Isaac Kook, (1865-1935), was a Torah prodigy known for his breadth of knowledge, mystical wisdom, profound poetry, and ability to connect with all kinds of Jews. He was an ardent Zionist who became the Chief Ashkenazic Rabbi of Palestine for the years, 1921-1935. He believed our settling the land of Israel will bring about the beginning of the messianic age.

The Kotzker Rebbe, (1787-1859), Rabbi Menachem Mendel of Kotzk, was a child prodigy of Talmud and Kabbalah. He became a Hasidic leader and the spiritual founder of the Ger tradition. He was known for his down-to-earth ideology, commitment to Truth, and the belief that each person needs to stretch their abilities to the absolute limit.

Davida Krauss, age 9. Davida's family in Israel is very important to her.

Zachy Krauss, age 7

Rabbi Aryeh Levin, (1885-1969), His great compassion and deep love for others fueled his passionate pursuit of charity and kindness, particularly for those in most unfortunate circumstances. His radiant love for each individual was magnetic, transformative, and legendary, touching the hearts of those near and far. He was a spiritual giant and great *tzaddik* (righteous person).

Rabbi Yisrael Lifshitz, (1782-1861), a French and German commentator on the Mishnah authored the authoritative commentary to the Mishnah — Tiferet Yisrael, The Glory of Israel.

Rabbi Judah Loew, The Maharal of Prague, (1525-1609), was an important Talmudic scholar, Jewish mystic, and philosopher. He developed a new approach to the *aggadah* (non-*halachic* thought of the rabbis) of the Talmud. This also opened a gate to Jewish mysticism, elucidating the deeper inner content of the Torah. He believed Jewish education should engage children in developmentally appropriate curriculum.

Maimonides, Moses ben Maimon, also known as Rambam, (1135-1204), was a rabbi, doctor, and philosopher. He composed works of Jewish scholarship as well as medical texts. Among many influential works was the Mishneh Torah in which he created a systematic code for all of Jewish law, guiding Jews in how to conduct themselves in various situations.

Alix Marson, age 14, is a passionate tennis player and is looking forward to college.

Daniella Marson, age 11, loves good writing and aspires to be a writer herself.

Jade Marson, age 11

Tamar Marson, age 14, loves Israel and plans to live there one day.

Rabbi Menachem Mendel of Rimanov, (1745-1815), was introduced to Hasidism at age 11. He became an important Hasidic leader in Poland. He was known for his extraordinary awe of God, his passionate prayer, and his reputation as a miracle worker. His writings were published posthumously.

Avital Mintz-Morgenthau, age 15.

Rabbi Nachman of Bratslav, (1771-1819), the grandson of the founder of Hasidism, the Baal Shem Tov, was himself a founder of the Breslover Hasidic sect. Central to his passionate teachings were the importance of prayer, particularly speaking to God from the heart, the critical role of the *tzaddik* in helping others transform themselves, and the message of finding hope and joy even in the darkest moments. His main work, *Likutey Moharan*, is a collection of sermons. He is also known for his stories which are based on kabbalistic thought (the mystical wisdom of Torah). After his death, no other Rebbe has filled his place as leader of the Breslovers.

Ari Naggar, age 9, loves basketball.

Drew Nuchims, age 6, loves Passover because he gets to see family he doesn't see much.

Tamar Padwa, age 6, loves to play football with her brothers.

Noa Pitkowsky, age 6, is proud that she was born in Israel and loves to read at night.

Miriam Shira Richter, age 9

Yitzy Richter, age 6, likes to be outside playing sports with people who have good sportsmanship.

Ariel Rosenberg, age 13, plays a mean guitar and enjoys watching great movies. He plans to win an Oscar one day.

Ayelet Rosenberg, age 9, keeps busy doing art, hanging out with her friends, and taking care of her many pets.

Elana Rosenthal, age 9

Dovie Rossman, age 16

Tzipporah Rossman, age 10, is passionate about Israel and enjoys spending time with her family and friends.

Yonah Rossman, age 12

Ezra Schwab, age 7, likes to learn anything.

Rabbi Chaim Shmuelevitz, (1902-1979), was the head of the Mir Yeshiva in Jerusalem for more than forty years. His erudition in Torah and his outstanding character made him one of the great Torah scholars of our generation, inspiring many. He wrote extensively and with penetrating insight on *mussar*, a Jewish ethical philosophy and spiritual discipline.

Yehuda Siegal, age 7

Zevi Siegal, age 13

Toba Stern, age 8, loves her family, friends, acting, and writing.

Rabbi Abraham J. Twerski, MD, is a prominent teacher, utilizing Torah teachings for self-improvement, and is a widely recognized authority in chemical dependency treatment. He is a psychiatrist, associate professor of psychiatry at the University of Pittsburgh School of Medicine, and a prolific author.

Gila Weinrib, age 7, loves to travel.

Avigayil Yucht, age 8, loves Am Yisrael, Eretz Yisrael, and Medinat Yisrael.

Rabbi Shneur Zalman of Liadi, (1745-1813), founded the Chabad Lubavitch sect of Hasidism. The word Chabad is an acronym for *chochma* (wisdom), *binah* (understanding), and *daat* (knowledge). In his magnum opus, *Tanya*, he outlined the Chabad philosophy and ethos. As well as being a Torah scholar, he also had extensive knowledge of mathematics and science.

Yona Zierler Feit, age 8, loves being with her family.

Amram Zeitchik, age 7, likes to talk about anything but finance.

Reb Zusha, Rabbi Meshulam Zusha of Anapoli, (1718-1800), was a major disciple of the Maggid of Mezritch (a successor to the Baal Shem Tov) and was among the most humble of men, an inspired and great sage and *tzaddik*. He combined self-effacing devotion and attachment to God with an ardent love for the Jewish people. His reflections and commentaries are compiled under the title, *Menorat Zahav*.

Acknowledgements

Exceptional people supported this work and I am happy to be able to thank them publicly. First, the children who exuberantly and with open hearts shared their thoughts and feelings with me about Pesach, and to their parents who supported their participation in this project.

To my beloved children and grandchildren, Tamar and Andy and Daniella, Ella and Micah, who fill my life with love, *nachat*, and meaning and who lead and share at *sedarim* with depth, kindness, and respect for every person at the seder table. To Merrill, my sister, who was there and is there at *sedarim* and in life. To dear friends, Rena Rossman, Yosepha Sarlin, and Robin Yucht who read early drafts of this manuscript with enthusiasm and kind, helpful eyes. To my dear teachers and friends, Rabbi Murray and Rena Schaum, and Rabbi Yamin Goldsmith who believed in the value of this work and helped shape it. To SAR Academy and our principal, Rabbi Binyamin Krauss, who leads a school without walls that is open to letting educators explore. Special thanks to my publishers, Larry and Eve Yudelson, who concretized this work in the world.

Rabbi Nachman of Bratslav said, "The exodus
from Egypt occurs in every human being, in every
era, in every year, and even in every day."

Similarly, Rabbi Shneur Zalman of Liadi
excluded from his Haggadah the passage,
"The order of the Passover seder is now concluded,"
because he understood that the seder's message continues all year.

We can leave Egypt every day by being conscious
to transcend that which limits us.

www.ingramcontent.com/pod-product-compliance
Lightning Source LLC
Chambersburg PA
CBHW081233090426
42738CB00016B/3278